STATIONS O

CORMAC RIGBY

FAMILY PUBLICATIONS

OXFORD

ISBN 978-1-871217-66-7

Art credits

Cover: St Michael & all Angels, Conway, Photo Michael Pitt-Payne
Page 1: Greyfriars, Oxford
Station I: Corpus Christi, Headington, Oxford
Station II: St Charles Borromeo, Ogle Street, London
Station III: Most Sacred Heart, Ruislip
Station IV: St Michael & all Angels, Conway, Photo Michael Pitt-Payne
Station V: Greyfriars, Oxford
Station VI: Ss Gregory and Augustine, Oxford
Station VII: Corpus Christi, Maiden Lane, London
Station VIII: Ss Anselm and Cecilia, Holborn, London
Station IX: Douai Abbey, Woolhampton
Station X: Carmelite Priory, Boars Hill
Station XI: St Brendan's Cathedral, Loughrea, Ireland
Station XII: Campion Hall, Oxford
Station XIII: Westminster Cathedral, London
Station XIV: Ramsgate Abbey, Photo Michael Pitt-Payne

published by

Family Publications
6a King Street, Oxford, OX2 6DF
www.familypublications.co.uk

printed in England

✠

At the beginning of each station:

We adore you O Christ and we bless you
Because by your holy Cross you have redeemed the world.

❧

At the conclusion of most stations (unless the Our
Father or Hail Mary are indicated):

I love you Jesus, my Love, above all things,
I repent with my whole heart for having offended you.
Never permit me to separate myself from you again.
Grant that I may love you always
And then do with me what you will.

❧

Between stations, a verse of the Stabat Mater, printed
underneath the illustration for each station.

At the Cross her station keeping,
Stood the mournful Mother weeping
Close to Jesus to the last.†

---

† Mediaeval hymn, possibly by Pope Innocent III, trans. Edward Caswall (1814-78).

First Station

Jesus is Condemned to Death

We adore you O Christ and we bless you
Because by your holy Cross you have redeemed the world.

Who was responsible for condemning Jesus to death? The Roman Governor, Pontius Pilate, was apparently the prime mover. But in fact, he would have preferred to distance himself. He would like to have been able to wash his hands of all responsibility for the prosecution of Jesus, which he could clearly see was not honestly motivated. It was not the alien occupying power that demanded death for Jesus. It was the local religious leaders, motivated not by justice but by jealousy. They ought to have seen Jesus as an ally against evil, but those chief priests were fearful of his influence.

Let us at this station recognise the corrosive power of jealousy. How many good people have been destroyed by resentment of other apparently 'good people'. Let us bear in mind all victims of envy, and especially all the victims of our own jealousy. We can't easily wash our hands of our own indifference, our own dubious motivation.

Our Father …

Jesus is laden with his Cross.

Through her heart His sorrow sharing
All His bitter anguish bearing,
Now at length the sword had passed.

JESUS RECEIVES THE CROSS

We adore you O Christ and we bless you
Because by your holy Cross you have redeemed the world.

There was nothing tidy and elegant in the death of Jesus. The Word of God made flesh was willing to accept the worst that life could fling at him.

And as he received the Cross, he knew he must stagger under its weight through crowds who only a few days earlier had been shouting 'Hosanna to the Son of David.' He went out to die as a criminal, not as a martyr. He had to endure scorn and rejection as well as his physical sufferings.

Let us at this station remember where we stand in the crowd. Do we go along with the mob? Do we allow ourselves to sink into that same sea of hatred and violence which in our own day and in our own country is still capable of drowning decency and love?

I love you Jesus, my Love, above all things ...

JESUS FALLS THE FIRST TIME UNDER HIS CROSS

O how sad and sore distressed
Was that Mother highly blessed,
Of the sole begotten One!

THIRD STATION

JESUS FALLS FOR THE FIRST TIME

We adore you O Christ and we bless you
Because by your holy Cross you have redeemed the world.

Jesus was weak from loss of blood, battered by the beating he
had received, blinded by the crown of thorns which had been
pressed on his head and ripped away again.
In his haze of pain he struggled under the weight of the Cross,
and his legs buckled under him, and he fell.

> Let us at this station understand that the Son of God who
> will sustain and strengthen us in our lives knows what it is
> to stumble and fall.
> Let us echo the words of the Psalmist:
>
> 'I waited, I waited for the Lord
> and he stooped down to me; he heard my cry.
> He drew me from the deadly pit, from the miry clay.
> He set my foot upon a rock, and made my footsteps firm.'
>
> Happy are they who put their trust in the fallen Saviour.

I love you Jesus, my Love, above all things ...

Christ above in torments hangs,
She beneath beholds the pangs
Of her dying glorious Son.

Fourth station

Jesus meets his Mother

We adore you O Christ and we bless you
Because by your holy Cross you have redeemed the world.

❧

As Jesus is roughly pulled to his feet again to resume his path
to the place of execution, the first person he sees is his mother.
Mary reaches out to help him, powerless. Her son looks into
her eyes and sees the love and the sorrow there. The prophecy
of Simeon, made when Mary brought her infant son to the
temple, had come true. 'A sword will pierce your own soul too.'

Let us at this station keep silence in the presence of hurt
too deep for tears. Let us think of the Mother of Sorrows
and her Son, so close on that crowded road, so cruelly
separated.

'In the Gardens of God, in the daylight divine
Show me thy Son, Mother, Mother of mine.'

❧

Hail Mary ...

Is there one who would not weep,
Whelmed in miseries so deep
Christ's dear Mother to behold?

THE CROSS IS LAID ON SIMON OF CYRENE

We adore you O Christ and we bless you
Because by your holy Cross you have redeemed the world.

Jesus was so exhausted they feared he would die before he reached his execution. So the Roman soldiers grabbed an unsuspecting stranger, up from the country, to help carry the Cross. His name was Simon. He comes into history because he simply happened to be there when the Lord passed by and had need of him. Did he protest; did he say: 'Why should I? It's got nothing to do with me.' Or did he see that tragic figure staggering under the Cross and feel his heart overflow with pity and compassion? And as he helped Jesus to carry the Cross, did he shed the weight of all his own sins, swept away by that Love he was helping?

> Let us at this station think of the chance moments of life when unexpectedly we look up and see the weary figure of Christ stumbling towards us. And let us pray for the grace to help carry his Cross.

I love you Jesus, my Love, above all things ...

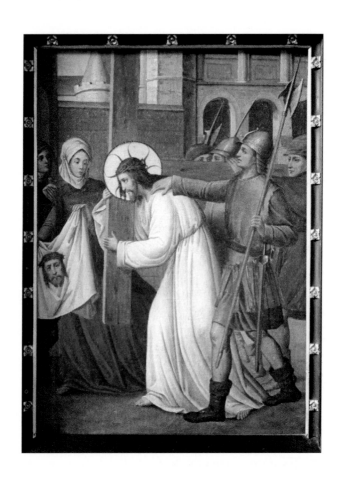

Can the human heart refrain
From partaking in her pain
In that Mother's pain untold?

VERONICA WIPES THE FACE OF JESUS

We adore you O Christ and we bless you
Because by your holy Cross you have redeemed the world.

❧

'Whose is this horrifying face,
This putrid flesh, discoloured, flayed,
Fed on by flies, scorched by the sun?
Whose are these hollow red-filmed eyes
And thorn-spiked head and spear-struck side?
Behold the Man: He is Man's son.'†

The image of the face of Jesus has haunted Christianity ever since that act of kindness on the road to Calvary when a woman called Veronica, seeing a fellow-creature so ill-used and bathed in sweat and blood, pressed a clean towel against his face.

Let us at this station be grateful to God for all the souls he has filled with compassion, souls who have gone to the aid of the suffering and who have carried away with them the image of the face of Jesus. Let us pray especially for all holy women of compassion, and find particular inspiration in the work begun by Mother Teresa of Calcutta.

❧

I love you Jesus, my Love, above all things ...

---

† The verse is the first verse of *Ecce Homo* by David Gascoyne (1916-2001).
From *Collected Poems*, OUP, London: 1965.

Bruised, derided, cursed, defiled.
She beheld her tender Child!
All with bloody scourges rent.

JESUS FALLS FOR THE SECOND TIME

We adore you O Christ and we bless you
Because by your holy Cross you have redeemed the world.

The physical collapse of Jesus is horrifying. The words of the Psalmist echo around him as he stumbles and falls a second time.

'Like water I am poured out; disjointed are all my bones.
My heart has become like wax; it is melted within my breast.
Parched as burnt clay is my throat; my tongue cleaves to my jaw.
Many dogs have surrounded me; a band of the wicked beset me;
they tear holes in my hands and my feet,
and lay in the dust of death.'

Let us at this station think of our Saviour
fallen a second time in the dust and dirt
of the street. Let us marvel that a man
should undergo all this and still be able
to find an excuse in his heart for those who
have so abused him. 'Father, forgive them;
they know not what they do.'

Our Father …

For the sins of His own nation
Saw Him hang in desolation
Till His spirit forth He sent.

THE WOMEN OF JERUSALEM WEEP FOR OUR LORD

We adore you O Christ and we bless you
Because by your holy Cross you have redeemed the world.

Even in the turmoil of this tortured ascent to Calvary, there are sparks of humanity. The women of Jerusalem identify with the mother who follows in the steps of Jesus, following him to the very foot of the Cross. They sense her sorrow and share it.

'Without beauty, without majesty we saw him, no looks to attract our eyes; a thing despised and rejected by men, a man of sorrows and acquainted with grief.'

Let us at this station understand what Jesus was saying to those compassionate women.
Gerard Manley Hopkins was moved that a child in autumn would grieve for the falling leaves, sensing not just the annual death of the tree but 'the blight man was born for,' that death that will come to us all.
Jesus sees his own death as the death of all humanity:
'Weep not for me, but for yourselves and your children.'

I love you Jesus, my Love, above all things ...

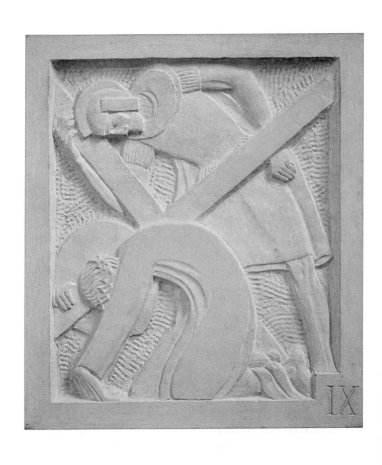

O thou Mother fount of love!
Touch my spirit from above,
Make my heart with thine accord.

JESUS FALLS FOR THE THIRD TIME

We adore you O Christ and we bless you
Because by your holy Cross you have redeemed the world.

❧

Truly Jesus was crushed for our sins. For
a third time he is borne down by his extreme
exhaustion, and even the brave efforts of Simon
of Cyrene cannot save him as he falls again.

'The enemy pursues my soul; he has crushed my
life to the ground; he has made me dwell in
darkness like the dead, long forgotten. Therefore
my spirit fails: my heart is numb within me.'

> Let us at this station promise Jesus that no matter how
> numb our hearts may be at the blows life has dealt us,
> we will always remember him struggling to his feet again
> to complete his mission of love. He was scarcely conscious,
> but his will drove him on – to offer his life for us.

❧

I love you Jesus, my Love, above all things ...

Make me feel as thou hast felt;
Make my soul to glow and melt
With the love of Christ my Lord.

JESUS IS STRIPPED OF HIS GARMENTS

We adore you O Christ and we bless you
Because by your holy Cross you have redeemed the world.

⨖

Clothes protect and give dignity to those who wear them. It is not uncommon for murderers to strip their victims and rob them of their dignity, as if to assert there is nothing more of value in a mere corpse. A lynch mob leaves its victims naked; the victims of the concentration camps went naked to the gas chambers; Our Lord was stripped. The sheer vulnerability of humanity becomes apparent; the ease with which life may be snuffed out.

Let us at this station contemplate that body now made visible. Let us see how the dignity of man cannot be denied by such callous brutality. The essence of man makes us vulnerable to death, victims of the bully, subject to power. But the beauty of God's creation is not to be extinguished by brute force. Vulnerable love is stronger than blind hatred; naked beauty is eternal, and violence is ultimately self-defeating.

⨖

I love you Jesus, my Love, above all things ...

Holy Mother! Pierce me through;
In my heart each wound renew
Of my Saviour crucified.

JESUS IS NAILED TO THE CROSS

We adore you O Christ and we bless you
Because by your holy Cross you have redeemed the world.

࿏

It was a scandalously cruel death. The executions of later ages at least tried to shorten the suffering. Beheading, shooting, hanging, electrocuting – all recognise the barbarity of prolonging the agony. Crucifixion was done deliberately to make suffering visible. And Christ's suffering has remained visible ever since. The sign of the Cross is not just a sign of death, but of suffering for love.

Let us at this station resolve to live always in the shadow of the Cross, to remember always that among those three crosses on Calvary, 'the midmost hangs for love.' Let the crucifix be with us always, through all our life and especially at our death.

'Hold thou thy Cross before my closing eyes;
shine through the gloom and point me to the skies;
heaven's morning breaks, and earth's vain shadows flee;
in life, in death, O Lord, abide with me.'†

࿏

I love you Jesus, my Love, above all things ...

---

† H F Lyte (1793-1847): *Abide with me.*

Let me share with thee His pain;
Who for all my sins was slain;
Who for me in torments died.

TWELFTH STATION

JESUS DIES ON THE CROSS

We adore you O Christ and we bless you
Because by your holy Cross you have redeemed the world.

'He had emptied himself, taking the form
of a servant, being born in the likeness of men.
And being found in human form, he humbled
himself and became obedient unto death,
even death on a cross. Therefore God has
exalted him, and bestowed on him the name
which is above every name, that at the
name of Jesus every knee shall bow, and
every tongue confess that Jesus Christ is Lord,
to the glory of God the Father.'†

Let us at this station recognise that it is accomplished.
Love has conquered all. Man is reconciled to God because
God has demonstrated that not even killing the Son of
God will deflect him from forgiveness. Death has no sting,
grave no victory, because Jesus Christ chose to die and
to rise again to new life.

Our Father …

---

† Phil, 2:9.

XIII. THE BODY OF JESUS IS TAKEN FROM THE CROSS AND LAID IN MARY'S BOSOM

Let me mingle tears with thee,
Mourning Him who mourn'd for me
All the days that I may live.

✠

JESUS IS TAKEN DOWN FROM THE CROSS

We adore you O Christ and we bless you
Because by your holy Cross you have redeemed the world.

The Pietà speaks in silence. The mother who held the babe in her arms in the stable at Bethlehem now holds the mangled body of her son. They stand around her, made silent by her sorrow. And silenced too by their own fear and failure. It is the darkest moment in Christianity. They had abandoned him; they believe his cause is lost. Christ is taken down from the Cross, and there is apparently no future for any of them. Only Mary is certain in her heart that somehow out of this terrible moment the angel's words are still valid. Hail full of grace, the Lord is with thee.

Let us at this station realise the full darkness of that hour, when every hope was gone, and death appeared to have had the last word. And let us gaze on the fearless sorrowing face of Mary.

Hail Mary …

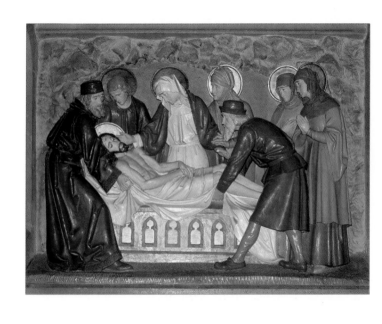

By the Cross with thee to stay;
There with thee to weep and pray,
Is all I ask of thee to give.

CHRIST IS LAID IN THE TOMB

We adore you O Christ and we bless you
Because by your holy Cross you have redeemed the world.

'If in that Syrian garden, ages slain,
You sleep, and know not you are dead in vain,
Nor even in dreams behold how dark and bright
Ascends in smoke and fire by day and night
The hate you died to quench and could but fan,
Sleep well and see no morning, son of man.

But if, the grave rent and the stone rolled by,
At the right hand of majesty on high
You sit, and sitting so remember yet
Your tears, your agony and bloody sweat,
Your cross and passion and the life you gave,
Bow hither out of heaven and see and save.'[†]

Let us at this station contemplate the great mystery of our faith,
the death of Jesus, and the empty tomb. Dead when the soldiers
came to investigate, so they did not break his bones, but pierced
his heart. Buried under guard. And after three days risen, to be
seen by Mary Magdalen in the garden on Easter morning.

Glory be …

† AE Housman (1859-1936): *Easter Hymn*, from *Collected Poems*, Jonathan Cape, London:
1939.

O Deus, ego amo te

O God, I love thee, I love thee –
Not out of hope of heaven for me
Nor fearing not to love and be
    In the everlasting burning.
Thou, thou, my Jesus, after me
    Didst reach thine arms out dying,
For my sake sufferedst nails and lance,
Mocked and marrèd countenance,
    Sorrows passing number,
    Sweat and care and cumber,
Yea, and death, and this for me,
    And thou couldst see me sinning:

Then I, why should not I love thee,
Jesu, so much in love with me?
Not for heaven's sake; not to be
Out of hell by loving thee;
Not for any gains I see;
But just the way that thou didst me
I do love and I will love thee:
What must I love thee, Lord, for then? –
For being my king and God. Amen.[†]

Our Father, Hail Mary, and *Glory be,* for the Holy Father

† Gerard Manley Hopkins: *The Poems of Gerard Manley Hopkins SJ*, Fourth Edition, Oxford University Press, London: 1918/1967.